OVERCOME ANXIETY IN RELATIONSHIPS

Create a meaningful relationship without harmful drugs and therapy

Wanda-Anne Downtoearthflower

any methods, procedures, or bearings embedded within it. No lawful obligation or default shall be made against the distributor for any reparation, damage, or money misfortune due to the information in this, either directly or implicitly.

Any copyrights not held by the seller are asserted by individual authors.

The data in this document is only available for educational purposes and is all-inclusive. The data are entered without a contract or confirmation of assurance.

The marks used shall be without consent, and the mark shall be distributed without the consent or support of the proprietor. All trademarks and trademarks in this book are for explanation only and are clearly held by owners who are not associated with the record.

Table of Contents

INTRODUCTION

WHAT IS ANXIETY?

Anxiety is the feeling that you have when you believe something unpleasant will happen in the future. Other words like *apprehensive*, *uncertain*, *nervous* and *on edge* also provide a good description of anxiety-related feelings.

Anxiety is entirely natural, and something that all human beings encounter from time to time when presented with challenging or threatening circumstances. The word 'anxiety' is frequently used to cover a wide range of feelings and is linked to emotions such as fear and concern. In reality, the words 'fear' and 'anxiety' are just about synonymous.

Anxiety in itself can be a helpful emotion, as it can help you prepare and improve your performance for events ahead. Anxiety, however, can sometimes become so severe and intense that it becomes debilitating and begins to restrict the daily routine or even life itself. Essentially, at that stage, the anxiety has got out of proportion, and you end up feeling much more depressed than you should, given your circumstances because you could be suffering from an anxiety disorder. Many different anxiety disorders exhibit symptoms of anxiety at their core.

What Triggers Anxiety?

Some people seem to have a propensity to be nervous, and new research shows that certain types of anxiety disorders might be inherited.

After witnessing multiple painful, upsetting experiences, or events in their lives, people develop anxiety disorders. For example divorce, bereavement, beginning a new career, moving to a new house, etc. may trigger anxiety.

Anxiety disorders can also be taught, especially after seeing someone else acting anxiously. It usually occurs when children see their parent/significant adult fearing something in their lives. For example, if the adult figure is afraid of spiders, the child will probably grow up fearing them as well, being familiar with that nervous behavior. There is no clear cause for their anxiety, however, for many people, and it's just something they create.

The following section of this guide goes into more

detail on the causes of anxiety.

How Did Anxiety Develop? Life Pressures – 'the Difficulties of Life'

People often find it very difficult to understand precisely where their anxiety comes from since there is not always a straightforward trigger. However, in my experience, I've found that most people develop anxiety after having been under 'stress' for some time and that a specific trigger is not necessarily present. You may have encountered loads of slight stresses that seem low by themselves. However, they accumulate, amounting to very considerable tension. Think back in the last few years: What were you going through? I know for myself that the cause for my anxiety encounter started when my house was burgled into and my car was stolen three months later. I then started to work in a secluded environment away from family and friends. At that time, I thought I had dealt with those setbacks successfully, but six months later, I started having panic attacks– probably a delayed reaction to stress. To experience anxiety, you don't even have to have suffered stressful, distinct events. For starters, you may have had an unpleasant boss at work to deal with for several years, and you have been slowly worn down by the tension and strain of that working relationship. This form of stress is called 'life pressure.' Another example would be to live consistently on the breadline: poverty is a well-known factor in a person's predisposition to anxiety.

Sometimes, there is confusion about the source of the anxiety. For instance, we've known many successful people in business, accustomed to flying regularly when all of a sudden they experience an anxiety attack during a flight. They then develop what they find to be a fear of flight. It is crucial to distinguish between a genuine fear of flying from an anxiety attack that has just happened while on an aircraft. In such situations, the individual concerned would have been depressed considerably for some time, more often than not. Unfortunately, this stress/anxiety came to a head when that person was traveling.

This scenario can be extended to include other specific fears. When I first began to have panic attacks, one of the first incidents occurred in a huge traffic jam. From there on, I made a conscious effort to avoid any road where I thought a jam might be possible. As you can see, I was wrong to associate the places I had an anxiety attack with the cause of the attack. Now I know the places and circumstances were completely insignificant, and it was the way I felt that fueled the terror. I was terrified of the anxiety attacks and had started living in the 'terror of terror' – a term you may have seen in many self-help books!

Specific Traumatic Incidents

If you feel that over the past year or so you have not been especially stressed out, it could be that anxiety began after a specific incident, known as a 'cause.' That is also a very common reason for anxiety to develop. After experiencing any of the following, we found that people are more likely to suffer from anxiety disorders: grief, divorce, moving to a new house, surgery, illness, or violence. Of course, there are other triggers, but these are typical and more common. Whether you have developed a more 'serious' phobia, such as claustrophobia, you could have been trapped in a lift or underground, and it is more possible that your current fear has been caused by this. Look back again to the incidents that have taken place in recent months. Did you encounter something at the time that caused you great anguish?

Certain people who during their childhood witnessts with them into adulthood, though they may have actively overlooked it. For instance, a child scared during a thunderstorm can grow up into an adult with an unreasonable fear of storms. Anxiety caused by specific triggers usually begins very soon after the trigger and is, therefore, easier to trace to its source. For example, a bad flight incident can immediately lead to anxiety about further air travel. Similarly, a traumatic experience at the dentist can lead to dental phobia. Social conditioning has to do with how you developed your anxiety disorder. Many people appear to be witnessing their anxiety from a family member or relative. How often do you learn that a person who's scared of spiders has a parent who's scared of them too? Even when we are kids, we subconsciously pick up prejudices from other people. We think this is because adults know best. If your mother is scared of spiders, that means spiders are dangerous to you as a child, and you should stay away from them. You can be able to trace the anxiety back to childhood, and therefore compensate for it.

The person with anxiety needs to be surrounded by

a safe environment where he/she can feel calm and can concentrate. Looking around and focusing on your surroundings rather than looking inwards and introverting is a very powerful remedy, so do not underestimate this. Daily long walks and communication with your environment can resolve your anxiety more than any therapy.

Medication has a lot of side effects and it can also be prescribed for imaginary illnesses. Anxiety is a psychosomatic manifestation so you don't need any psychological drugs to make you better. They will only worsen your condition. If you want to resolve anxiety find out what is the Reactive Mind and how it causes your psychosomatic anxiety. Read the bestseller *Dianetics* by L. Ron Hubbard, it has helped millions of people to resolve their anxiety issues and understand what is the source of it.

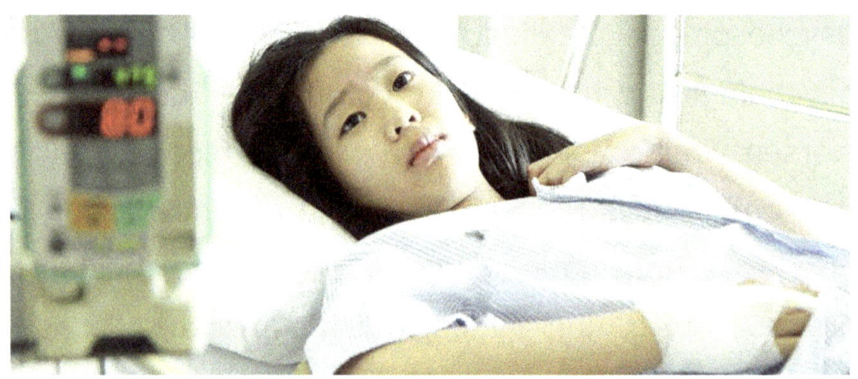

UNDERSTANDING ANXIETY

So, you spent some time thinking back about your life trying to identify the source of your anxiety. Don't worry if you still feel like you can't figure out where it comes from. Many people believe that even though you know the root of anxiety and how it came about, it is basically useless when attempting to cope with the actual issues you face.

To understand anxiety and start controlling it, you have to separate anxiety into three separate aspects:

Physical Aspects of Anxiety

When you are placed in an anxiety-provoking situation, an automatic chain of events begins, often known as the 'fight or flight' response. This reaction happens without us thinking about it, as it is activated by the part of our nervous system that regulates our automatic functions (e.g. breathing, heartbeat, etc.). This portion of our nervous system is called the 'autonomic system' and is divided into two components: parasympathetic and sympathetic. Those functions are opposite and only one can be dominant at a time. Our sympathetic system starts to dominate when we are in some situation that causes us anxiety and the 'fight or flight' response starts (also known as the 'adrenaline cascade').

The step-by-step cycle below shows what occurs when the sympathetic system is activated: the hormone adrenaline is released into the bloodstream.

The heart beats faster to rapidly circulate blood throughout the body and provide energy to the muscles to allow them to prepare for 'fight or flight.' Blood is redirected from areas of the body where it is not needed – for example, away from the stomach. This is why when we're nervous, we sometimes experience a churning sensation in the stomach also known as 'butterflies.'

Now the heart pumps more forcefully, which is linked to an increase in blood pressure. It's this increase in blood pressure that makes us feel dizzy and light-headed.

Consequently, there's also a temperature increase. Your body is responding by trying to cool you down.

That system is designed to serve us in real-life danger. The problem becomes when our system is 'turned on' when we don't really need it because we aren't in a life-threatening situation. When this cascade of events is turned on for no apparent reason, we feel even worse.

I experienced this myself after suffering panic attacks for a month or so. Suddenly, without excuse, I started getting those attacks. I'd be watching TV, relaxing when one would hit me full-on. I was even more worried, like many people, because now, for no obvious reason, I felt fearful. What I now know is that my concern about the panic attacks coming out of the blue actually served to increase my overall tension and anxiety levels. And my panic level fell dramatically – with the result that only tiny incidents might set me off.

It's probably helpful for you to see a list of some of the physical symptoms of anxiety at this point because these symptoms are not in your head. On the contrary, they are very real and triggered by the adrenaline release: butterflies in your stomach, shortness of breath, headaches, dizziness, hot flushes, increased breathing, alertness, dry mouth, tightness around the chest, etc.

None of these symptoms is pleasant, so people trying to avoid them is quite understandable. But avoidance only serves to reinforce our fears, as you will read later.

Many of the physical signs encountered by people in the middle of an anxiety disorder and often misinterpreted include a fast pulse that is perceived as a sign of an impending heart attack and butterflies in the stomach that is believed to be a sign of vomiting.

In fact, over the years we have been approached by a lot of people who told us they had to rush off to the emergency room because they really thought they had a heart attack. Once there, they were told that their problem was entirely psychosomatic (when the mind effects the body). I had a colleague driving home from university one night, who had a heart attack. He was so terrified he sped frenzied to the next turn off and ran into a café, thinking he was dying. The lady on the till of course did not know he wasn't, and called an ambulance. Four hours later, my friend was left on a sideward blowing into a paper bag, after exhaustive medical tests! There was nothing wrong with him physically. Instead, he responded to the physical symptoms of his anxiety – misinterpreting the rapid heartbeat that goes hand in hand with anxiety as a sign that something with his heart was wrong. This is a generalization but, over the years, it appears that women are generally more concerned about being sick, while men are more concerned about the physical symptoms of anxiety that affect the heart. Being sick as a woman was a big issue for me. I don't know what it really was about. I can only assume that I had this belief somewhere in my mind that being sick was socially unacceptable, and certainly not something a woman should be doing in public. Looking back, there seemed to be a bit of a stigma attached to the public illness. Only after experiencing extreme morning sickness strikes in both of my pregnancies did I come to acknowledge that there are worse things to do than being sick on the ground!

Of course, other physical symptoms bother people like profuse sweating, shaking, blushing, and so on. These physiological symptoms of anxiety seem to cause distress to those with social phobia – an anxiety condition in which people worry that their anxiety may be noticeable to others.

I would point out that while the physical symptoms encountered during anxiety attacks are mostly due to anxiety, in most cases it is still necessary to see your GP first of all and to disregard any medical conditions such as thyroid disorder, perimenopausal symptoms, etc. Besides preparing the body for physical action, adrenaline often mentally motivates us to do something about the condition which has triggered this enormous release of adrenaline to occur. You can also describe the symptoms as what you think, feel, and say to yourself when you're anxious.

Here's a list of common thoughts and emotions that people feel when they are anxious:

- Feeling scared and panicky.

- Worrying you may lose control and/or go 'crazy.'

- Worrying you might die.

- Thinking you may have a heart attack/ brain tumor.

- Thinking you may get sick, faint, or embarrass yourself.

- Sensing people watching you, witnessing your fear.

- Generally feeling as though things are accelerating.

- Feeling separated from your environment and the people in it.

- Feeling like running away/escape from the situation.

- Feeling on edge.

The next time you experience an anxiety attack, it

could prove helpful to write down what you feel and think. Alternatively, you may want to record on your mobile phone with this information so you can capture the thoughts as they occur. You are likely to experience the same thoughts and feelings, or a variation on them, whenever you experience panic/anxiety—most people do. What you'll find is that your thoughts are almost always negative, and you've got into a thinking pattern where you believe the worst will happen. Likewise, when you look back on an anxiety attack and get things out of all proportion – seeing things in black or white, not shades of grey, you would definitely continue to catastrophize incidents.

As well as feeling nervous and panicky, you'll probably still be worrying about what's happening to you and might start imagining the worst. Such thoughts serve only to intensify the initial anxiety and fuel the adrenaline response. An anxiety disorder can quite easily be caused by thinking about anxiety symptoms. Before they even get there, many people make the mistake of imagining what they would feel like in a situation. Apart from being usually much worse than the event itself, this 'anticipatory anxiety' only serves to prime the body to experience 'panic.' It explains why those of us who are agoraphobic will not be able to go out on a day-out that was arranged some time in advance and yet would go out on the spur of the moment. Most nervous people loathe meetings, and fear being backed into a corner.

For those with anxiety, advance notice will mean weeks of anticipatory anxiety and depressive thoughts.

When you think back to your last bout of anxiety, you might find it beneficial what it was that you were really scared of. This is also better said than done, though, so you will need help with this – we'll provide suggestions later in this guide on where to get help. But, as we mentioned before, you can always take long walks and put your attention on the physical objects around you. This helps to get immediately extroverted.

Behavioral Aspects of Anxiety

Symptoms are what we do when we are anxious – that is, our response to our thoughts, feelings, and physical symptoms. Anxiety's most common behavioral symptom is avoidance. How many times have you stopped putting yourself in a situation you feel nervous about? DON'T for all of you who haven't evaded circumstances! Evasion serves only to reinforce the message of risk, and while at the moment, it can seem to feel the right thing to do, it is just a short-term solution. Likewise, often an anxious person has avoided a situation where they begin to feel nervous. From my own experience, I found that when I ran away from somewhere, it was always twice as hard as ever to go back home. Even if staying there is difficult when you feel utterly awful, do your best to fight the temptation to run. This doesn't mean that you're going to have to go in hell – you can always go for a stroll, refresh yourself in the bathroom – but it does mean sitting in position before the fear subsides and it does.

Think back through the past week, and recognize potential avoidance behaviors that you might have done. Below are some examples of avoidance behaviors: Taking taxis instead of using public transport or walking.

Create reasons to avoid having to go out with friends and relatives.

Sitting in theatres or cinemas at the end of a row.

Inviting going out alone; having someone with you always.

Rushing from circumstances where you are feeling nervous.

Shopping only when it's quiet.

To avoid busier ones and heavy traffic, using the smaller highways.

Cross the lane, to stop traffic.

You can always help yourself if you have already started avoiding those locations, doing different stuff, don't worry. The easiest way to do so is to set realistic goals for yourself, the ones that you can easily meet, and you can eventually face the situation that causes you anxiety. While some people believe they need to receive advice from a specialist, it's possible to do this yourself.

If you feel confident enough to embark on a desensitization program alone, then it is a good idea to write down a hierarchy of tasks to complete over a period of time that you would like to commit yourself to. The first task on the list will be something you would consider reasonably straightforward to do, and the last task is something you wouldn't imagine but would like to do if you weren't stressed at the moment. My list had looked like this at the time:

1. Go to the post box four doors away.

2. Go to the corner shop.

3. Stand in the post office queue when quiet.

4. Stand in the post office queue when busy.

5. Go to the supermarket.

6. Do all the above in sequence but alone.

7. Do all the above in sequence but walk, not take the car.

8. Go to the local shopping mall.

9. Go into Manchester city center.

10. Go beyond Manchester city center.

In the beginning, it is important to set yourself small tasks that are easily accomplished. If you're giving yourself things that are too hard or risky, you just set yourself up to fail. Of course, doing the above alone never suffices. You will also need to practice relaxation, implement positive thinking, and other strategies for handling anxiety to be able to be fully effective and continue on the all-important 'path to recovery.'

Anxiety Management

As you would have seen from the personal accounts of anxiety provided, while the concepts of anxiety are the same, people are separate entities and consider different variations of beneficial approaches when it comes to controlling their anxiety.

So now that we've looked at the three components of anxiety — the physical,

logical, and behavioral aspects — we're going to look at coping mechanisms and how to control anxiety. There are various approaches to treat anxiety – each tailored to deal with one of the three components: Relaxation therapy is usually effective when coping with anxiety's physical symptoms. Thought-stopping strategies and extroversion are useful ways to overcome bad symptoms, and help you treat avoidance patterns that you might have established along the way. You could use all of these techniques yourself and be able to practice them alone without spending any money! Relaxation therapy is a technique aimed at decreasing physical stress in the body which has formed as a result of anxiety and requires daily exercising. There are variations on the relaxation theme but most concentrate on each body's muscle group, alternating between stress and relaxation. When this is performed over the whole body, the total muscle tension of an individual would be significantly reduced. Relaxation exercise also tends to reduce heart rate and blood pressure, and slow breathing rate. People often experience an 'inner tranquility' sensation.

Relaxation works by assisting you to let go of any anxiety you have endured. Most of us with anxiety disorders seek to control the fear by keeping ourselves in a tight, tight manner. We feel like we might only panic if we let go. This couldn't be further from the truth, unfortunately. We just contribute to the current level of anxiety in our body by staying continuously stressed and making it more likely for a panic attack to occur.

Also, if you get into a state of relaxation before a situation you feel is going to cause you anxiety, it will be truly harder for you to get worked up later! At this point, it is important to mention breathing, as many people with anxiety tend to over breathe, or hyperventilate. Though anxious people tend to breathe more, they are starting to develop defective breathing patterns. You are most likely to have entered into a breathing pattern whereby you take your oxygen from the top of your lungs, which leads to your shoulders moving up and down. You should use your lower abdomen for breathing properly, and your tummy should rise and fall gently with each breath. Place your hand on your tummy to see if your tummy is rising and falling to test if you are breathing correctly (well funny this can sound). If not, it's most likely you've learned the nervous technique of breathing – taking lots of quick, short breaths from the upper torso, instead of deep, long breaths from the lower abdomen.

Normal respiration is so necessary to regulate anxiety.

Breathing is a lot more than just taking in a gasp of air – the proportions of very important gases in our blood are regulated at each breath. Changing the balance of these gasses will cause you to feel light-headed, dizzy, and surreal. Many people find that their anxiety symptoms dramatically decrease just by correcting their breathing, so it's important to rectify faulty breathing early.

However, it is important to note that hyperventilation is nothing to worry about in itself and will not harm you. It is just like anxiety in fact – unpleasant, but harmless.

Try this exercise at breathing deep now.

Deep Breathing Exercise

- Slowly breathe via the nose for a count of 3

- As you inhale, push your tummy out for a count of three

- Hold out for a count of 3

- Exhale via your mouth for a count of five

- As you breathe out, pull your tummy out for a time. Be sure that you're in a quiet room, where you won't get upset. Reading the exercise and recording it so you can listen with your eyes closed while lying down may be helpful. With anything new, it would take some time for you to learn to relax, but the exercises will become second nature in time.

Relaxing Workout

- Emphasis on your feet. Scrunch your toes firmly, and stay for three counts. Relax the feet, and uncurl.

Repeat twice on this.

- Stick to your feet. Move downward the sole of your foot. Feel the stress. Keep three for a count, and then relax.

Repeat twice on this.

• Contract the muscles in your thighs and stay for three seconds, then relax.

Repeat twice on this.

• Tighten your bottom muscles and hold for a count of 3, then relax.

Repeat twice.

• Hold your tummy lightly in by a deep breath for a count of three. Hold out a big breath and release your tummy.

Repeat twice on this.

• Raise your hands to your ears and stay for three, then relax.

Repeat twice on this.

• Scrunch your eyes tightly, stay for three counts, and relax.

Repeat twice on this.

• Roll now in a relaxed place and keep your eyes closed for five minutes.

• At the end of the workout, stretch softly, then

gradually get up.

You may want to play soothing music CDs while practicing calming techniques – such as those featuring seawater, dolphin sounds, and falling rain. In addition to burning essential oils like lavender, geranium, etc., some people find it useful.

The following approaches are intended to help you cope with the anxiety symptoms.

Distraction Techniques

These techniques aim at getting you to think about something else instead of your anxious thoughts. Distraction is very useful to practice in situations where you feel confined – for instance while waiting in a queue in a supermarket or stuck in a jam! Instead of thinking thoughts like, 'I have to get out of here, I feel panicky,' look at the surroundings – look at the people in the queue, what they wear, what they purchase. One of my friends used to imagine curly pink-haired boys! This would help her have a little laugh to herself, and succeed in changing the focus from negative to positive in her thoughts.

Whenever you make a positive effort to stop thinking

anxiously, you would be surprised at what you can think of!

There are other ways to relax, which you might find helpful too.

These are

• Counting from 100 backward in groups of 3s

• Reading the English alphabets backward If you consider these boring or too simple, you might formulate your diversion strategies!

Self-Talk

You could also learn to control anxious thoughts in an anxiety-provoking situation by talking yourself. By now, you should've written down all the thoughts that come back every time you feel anxious, and so you'll be familiar with them. You know from reading this guide's earlier segment that these thoughts just wind you up more, and make the anxiety worse. So, these thoughts need to be replaced with positive, more balanced ones. Look at your list of negative thoughts, now-write a POSITIVE answer for each one. For instance, if your negative thought is, 'I can't cope, I'm going to have a heart attack,' your response will be,

'I've coped before, and now that I've learned more coping mechanisms, I'm going to do better.' I realize I'm not going to have a heart attack because it's just adrenaline that makes my heart pump faster. This is a normal reaction to a cycle of a human body.

Give yourself credit for getting through the anxiety at the end of this process, and not allow it to overwhelm you completely. Each time you practice, it'll get easier. Finally, when you are not feeling anxious, it is important to practice coping skills thoroughly, and then put them into play in a real-life situation. Your goal is also to learn how to control the anxiety, NOT to get rid of it.

Postponing Worry

This is a technique that focuses on 'postponing worry' rather than attempting to suppress worrying thoughts. Instead of listening to distracting and worrying thoughts as they happen spontaneously during the day, assign a particular time and place to think about. Whenever worrying thoughts pop up outside of this time, you simply note the type of worry (although it's not always necessary); classify the thought into, for example, 'working worrying thoughts,' 'home worrying thoughts,' 'relationships worrying thoughts.' Then, during the allocated worry time, you should come back to these thoughts and say to yourself: "I'm not going to think about this now, I'm going to come back to it during my worry time." This cycle would get simpler over time and ultimately get a habit. Returning to worries when you're in a more relaxed frame of mind will often result in the 'worries' appearing less problematic and related to the point that you find it easier to solve problems or simply re-evaluate the worries, categorizing them as less important and therefore less troubling.

What Else Can Help?

Diet

Try eating a healthy, sensible diet. This is significant because fluctuating blood sugar levels can trigger the same symptoms like anxiety, which are often the product of snacking and not consuming healthy meals.

Therefore, it is advisable for that immediate sugar fixes and turns to consume foods that will give you a more steady sugar release. Carbohydrate foods – bread, rice, cereals, and pasta – in particular, whole grain carbohydrates are very good at this.

Take off caffeine from your diet. Caffeine increases symptoms of anxiety, especially palpitations, a jumpy feeling, and shakiness. Caffeine can also be found in tea, chocolate, and some beverages aside coffee. Caffeine-free alternatives of most drinks are now available, and you don't have to cut them from your diet, just turn to decaffeinated versions!

Cut on alcohol consumption too. Many people notice that they feel much more depressed the day after they've had a beer, and that's not connected, it seems to any hangover they might have too. This is often referred to as a 'hangover of fear.' Excess alcohol will make you more susceptible to the stress effects.

Cut back on smoking or quit. Nicotine and some other chemicals found in cigarettes increase anxiety symptoms by boosting heart rate and blood pressure. Herbal, homeopathic and natural remedies Please note: you should always check with your GP and/or pharmacist before embarking on any natural/herbal remedies as some may interfere and interact with prescription medicines that you might take.

In the United States, the herb, St, John's Wort has often been identified as 'nature's relaxant.' It's known to support people with mild to moderate depression and anxiety and can help restore a relaxed inner feeling. It's common in many health food stores.

Stress-relieving herbal tablets are now available. Looking at the back of herbal tablet packages and testing the content is a good idea. Chamomile and Lemongrass are important herbs because when they're boiled and drunk as a tea, they give out a pleasant feeling.

Homeopathic treatments may also be able to tackle anxiety disorders. A large array of homeopathic treatments for a range of conditions are available now.

Bach Rescue Remedy is a combination of 5 flower essences, which are taken in the form of a liquid droplet under the tongue when anxious. Some people swear by this treatment and have their bottle ready at all times!

Aromatherapy, therapeutic massage, acupuncture, and other interventions have been used to relieve/reduce anxiety symptoms.

Physical Exercise

It is difficult to ignore the fact that not only is physical exercise excellent to keep us safe, it also keeps us mentally strong. There have also been several studies that has found physical exercise to be one of the most successful ways to boost self-esteem. This explanation is thought to be as a result of exercise that induces the release of the body's natural endorphins, while also increasing chemical transmission such as serotonin. Any exercise will help lower your stress levels, and therefore help regulate your anxiety. Many people who have asked for help with anxiety have found that swimming, running, walking, and yoga are particularly helpful. I have heard people with agoraphobia claim they were helped tremendously by riding a bicycle. Physical exercise is believed to use the excess dopamine in their bodies that anxiety sufferers have, and so it is always worth persisting even though you are not naturally inclined to engage in sport. Community support Having contact with others is key to recovery, I believe. Isolating yourself from your worries only worsens matters. This is why peer support on a person's path to recovery from anxiety is so critical.

Self-Help Groups

One of the things that I found most helpful when I first started anxiously struggling was finding someone who knew exactly what I was going through. I launched my own self-help community in Manchester because shockingly there was nothing for people like me in that big city at the time! A lot of self-help groups are now in service across the world.

Mentors are not therapists but individuals who are able to listen to your problems and help you in discussing the issues that most concern you. A mentor may support you by:

- Enhancing mental and emotional well-being

- Boost your confidence

- Signposting to training, education, or job services

- Listening to your concerns to help you find ways to help relieve your worries

- Introduce you to a Pen pal scheme. Pen pal scheme helps people to write to/mail others and make friends. This service represents a good way to break any loneliness you might experience.

NEGATIVE THINKING IN RELATIONSHIPS

How your Negative Thoughts Could Be Ruining your Relationship

A relationship is as much physical as it is mental. The thought and mental well-being of your partner is a lot related to the relationship's success. It's not only what you say, but also what you think has the strength that most people don't understand. The thoughts that you have about your partner may affect the outcome of your relationship.

Start with yourself: I will tell you the importance of understanding yourself before we discuss how your negative thoughts might destroy your relationship. The very important thing in life is that your soul is strongly connected. Life truly reflects your inner condition. The people you attract represent who you are on inside so that through what you do not like you can know more about yourself. You get closer to understanding your worth and what you deserve by finding dislikes. You begin to understand how meaningful the inner reality is when you know who you are. You will know that when you are filled with the love you get from the unlimited source, you will be able to fill the person you love without hesitation. There's no correlation in trying to force or make you happy somebody to love you a certain way. You know these things begin with you.

Hidden thoughts hurt relationships: In addition to the multiple obstacles facing people when they maintain a healthy relationship, many links fail because of negative and terrible inner ideas. If you have learned the value of positive thinking, emotional expression, and communication, then the thought of your partner can either help or hurt your relationship. Say, your partner upsets you and pretends you "go over it," externally, but in your mind, you replay endlessly, with anger, annoyance, anxiety, sorrow, or sheer frustration, what he or she has done for you. You may have an internal dialogue saying, "they will do it again" or "why do they want to do this" or any other negative, recurring thoughts. You look nice on the outside, but you're upset about them internally. This shielding from real feelings begins to develop, leading to problems in the relationship. Through any emotional expression and communication do not solve problems, it leads to the couple's downfall and inevitably to the end of the relationship.

Seeking the solution: The most important thing is

how powerful these silent ideas can be. Why not heal with your mind instead of breaking down each other? What you think about your partner, they are, is a great awareness to have. You can know more about, or do not like, the features, practices, beliefs, and actions you do. It all depends where you put your mind and resources into thought. Build your partner's safe feelings, tell yourself sweet, loving words. Enjoy your smallest endeavor, tell them how you feel and how articulate you are. Think of them when you fall in love for the first time. Ask yourself, do I want to manifest this in my relationship, when you have a negative thought about it?

Be mindful: The whole relationship is pure thinking, and every thinking you send out can be a powerful energy that can align you and your partner to make the relationship healthier. You must manifest the fantasies of your spouse. Be sure you're aware of what you think and feel inside about them. Don't allow other people to control your thinking. People who don't know the strength of their feelings, words, and emotions seem to struggle to keep their relationship healthy. Note also that you're going to see what you think internally. Can your relationship be strengthened by passion?

All sorts of things can make a very good relationship ruinous. For example, two major ones are trickery and incompatibility. And the best way to resolve all problems is more communication. When you have a problem, MORE communication is always the solution, not LESS.

Think of the First Time you Fell in Love

It is easy to allow this cloud to judge when you go through a rough patch. When you start to think about the uncertainty of your partner's "true" feelings, think about how much you fell in love with them and how. "If the bright-eyed person you have fallen in love with closes your eyes, things will look even more hopeful and feasible." Often we need just a little reminder of the good times to resolve the evil.

It is easier said than done, to be honest, to let go of the past.

Separate the Past from the Present

"To somehow 'protect' us from being hurt again, all of us keep a piece of our past with us,". "But if you continue bringing your old relationships in your new one and the hurt along with it, you sabotage yourself and create the truth, that it's just not going to work.". "Do not presume that you know how they feel." If you are angry with your partner, having one go-to-person to slip through your relationship is not unusual for anyone who hears all of your problems.

Make a Record of your Toxic Ideas and Come up With Good Options.

Preventing toxic thoughts from destruction will take some self-reflection with constructive alternatives. One of the good things you can do during learning is to literally write down all the usual thoughts that help challenges or breaks. Take it a step further then write down hard evidence or facts against every proposal. Then come up with a more reliable and adaptive alternative POSITIVE thinking. For example, if you think your partner is no longer interested because they have not answered your text, list all the other things they could do.

Take Breaking Up off the Table

Whatever the toxic thoughts, usually the same place

— fear. Take Breaking Up In particular, the worry that you will abandon your partner. If there is no other alternative, you can start seeing the good in a situation. You can get to know your relationship from a place of love and not fear by the opportunity to break out from the equivalent. It will be easier for you to be optimistic if your words and actions come from a place of affection.

A thought is only a thought at the end of the day. It doesn't have to be the case. Your relationship is going to be much better for it if you do not permit it to overtake you.

You might think twice before you take yourself down or put excess negative effects and strain on your relationship if you're looking for love (like most of us are). You would like to be more optimistic about your behavior if you are trying to find a real relationship. It means that you're going to have to be more optimistic, and want to be open to love and to be real, where you know just how deserving of it. You could lose out on something that might be great down the road when you begin to put fear, doubt, reservation, and a fake character.

As a certified health coach, I work with our customers

to find happiness in their relationships. Of course, when you are honest, the good and the bad in terms of thinking and feelings must be shared, so you're better prepared to take everything into your partner. Yet if you're always bitter or pissed, it may be too much to deal with, especially if you know that you hold resentment or that you allow stuff to last too long.

Furthermore, there are not only negative thoughts you can remember around a new partner, but the negative thinking you might have might keep you from putting yourself there first. You won't have a fair chance of finding love and matching with somebody if there is too much uncertainty or doubt. The crap? Know when to keep negative feelings with yourself and when to turn bad ideas into positive ones to improve mental health.. "You have to love yourself and be whole as if you want to open up for someone else. "You're already done! The foundations for a healthy relationship are not two halves that build a whole. Two whole people gather to make a wonderful couple," explained Feinblatt.

I Don't Want to Lose that One

"This idea generates an illusion of perfection, that there is a perfect person for you. It puts a great deal of pressure on you to get that person." Rather, go in with openness and see how things are going, without any worry." Enjoy your relationship's beauty and joy. Setting out your ideal partner on the basis of assumptions or desires that restrict your potential for happiness. "If this is the right guy, then being your true self will never mess up. It just means it wasn't working out and you are both not compatible. Breakdowns, as they arise, are the reason for new developments. Avoid mistrust and lack of contact, and fear of involvement,"

This is apparent if the partnership is not intended to move forward. Don't repress your real and honest self, because that's just going to come out later. Be free. Be safe. Be daring. Be daring. You are out of my league. "You can screw up a relationship that could be perfect if you are constantly in question about your own worth. "It also calls into question the judgement of you in being first and foremost with you," Julie Wadley, licensed coach and matchmaker says on Bustle. "However, this is an incentive for a deceptive partner to go throughout you," adds Wadley. "I can turn it around." It is hard to learn the true one, if you always think you're used to it for yourself, you consider all of the efforts you make for them to be the person you wish they were, will be collected by the next one who embraces them as they are," said Wadley. And you get upset, on the other hand, over the grounds when they refuse to change. No one wins. Just because you don't think your beloved will or will not do things you don't like, doesn't mean he doesn't love you. "It will ruin the relationship that views this way," says Mitzi Bockmann, the Women's Accredited Life Coach, by email with Bustle.

"I Wonder How Their ex is."

Never ask, for example, about the other. It's human nature to be curious about who our partners have previously dated, but this offers nothing constructive and only wastes your time. There was a reason they didn't work things out. Sasha Bracha Bregman, a specialist in matchmaking and partnership in the NYC co-founder of Elite & Discreet, explains via email to Bustle that the passage is not applicable at all, "explains.

"Maybe I'm Meant to Be the Single Person."

That could be the case if you'd be happier, but don't believe this is your destiny without trying." 'If the way you tried it doesn't happen to you, take a break. Act on yourself. Work on yourself.

"Do they see somebody on the side?" "You know that you want to be with someone for a long time. Do they see others on the side of the people? "Even though you don't have to go on a day or second and commit for a long period of time (if the other one does so too early, it could be a red flag), you can make your beliefs and intentions quietly known to the third day. "Simply be genuine, say something such as 'I'll dig out the connection we have. By the 5th day, whether you are entering a monogamous relationship or still 'seeing' each other, it should be established,".

"Monogamy and Commitments Just Do not Work."

Relating to a negative attitude will make the other individual think you do not want to be monogamous actually and will not consider you to be a potential long-term partner. Set this as a goal and note some pseudo-trending and fads in the everyday world if you are looking for a long-term connection. "Be honest and genuine: Trust me we need more of this in the world,"

Be open to new relationships and trust that you will find the person to be the right person in time, one who understands the reality, if you are hitting the dating scene, you could set yourself up for failure.

Getting over Relationship Insecurity

There are moments when you believe you're not good enough, even though you think you've met the love of your life. Often you also experience those bouts of insecurity that not only cause an argument between you and your significant other, but also damage your self-esteem.

People who are not aware of their worth as an individual, a lover and a life partner, often experience insecurities in a relationship. However, some practices can help anyone who suffers from this negative emotional wave by following and believing in the various ways of overcoming uncertainties, especially in romantic relations.

So what are the steps you should be taking to make your partnership feel more secure? They are here.

1. **Stop Comparing Yourself to Others.**

Particularly former lovers of your significant other. It is one of the causes of problems between spouses, and while it can be natural and sometimes rational, some still find a way to make it an issue even though the triggers are in sight nowhere.

Insecurity and jealousy are a lethal combination, and how couples can either make or break the relationship in solving the problems that come with this combo.

2. **Start to Understand your Own Singularity**.

You are special, and not like anyone else. Keep that in mind. Some people, though, struggle to recognize the positive stuff about them and they always seem to despise themselves simply because they don't believe they're different. This is another indicator of vulnerability, which is the most growing.

Realizing that there are people who appreciate your mere existence is the best way to overcome this self-hatred. Secondly, and most importantly, there's someone beside you who loves you exactly as you are.

3. **Don't Be Afraid to Make the Proper Enquiries.**

The response, which we fear so much, from the questions we do not even dare put – due to lack of confidence and low self-esteem – has something to do with the reality at the roots of insecurity.

Often the desire to know the truth about the things that define us as a person and a lover can lead to confusion, anxiety, and sometimes overthink.

4. **Build Confidence**

Occasionally, the root cause of insecurity is not about what somebody doesn't have but about their inability to see what's already in front of them: their talents and their own goodness, which were the reasons that somebody fell in love with them first. And what is the only way of curing this 'blindness'? Rest assured.

Believe in yourself, and let faith scare away those

insecurities. How? How? There are numerous ways to be confident and proud of who you are and what you are. Everything you need to do is have the courage to open your eyes.

5. Accept More Men.

Another cause of the vulnerability is our inability to trust others due to past experiences that led us to believe you can't depend on someone but yourself. Let those go, and be open in your life to new people, build your community, and be with your crowd.

Stop building those walls, thinking it'll protect you from the outside world's cruelty. Alternatively, open more doors, open more windows, and you can brighten up your life through the light of others.

6. Find out What Really Troubles you.

We have listed several causes of insecurity in a relationship, particularly for women. Most of the more common reasons a person may feel insecure, however, really depend on a variety of factors.

Find out what really troubles you. Find the causes of things and situations that can make you experience these negativities. To put it another way, know yourself better, especially the bad parts.

7. Accept Things you Can't change.

Don't grieve about things you can never get back into, the realities you can't change in your relationship. Our inability to understand that the problems we see and face with your significant other are part of life is one of the causes of insecurities. You can still do better, though.

Start by seeing yourself and responding to the challenges, events, and interactions that come your way—responding in anger? Dwelling in anxiety? Or are you accepting them with a sort of maturity that can help you survive and cope?

8. Change your Attitude Toward People and to Life.

If you think nothing is improving in relation to the previous section, and you still feel disappointment and frustration in your relationship, maybe all you need is a change of perspective? If you don't like your reality as the popular saying goes, change it; if it doesn't work, change your attitude.

We understand it's easier to say than done, but we must all start somewhere, right? Now do it.

9. Find and Grow your Strengths

Instead of dwelling on the bad and the negative, find something you can build and draw power from inside you. For example, as a partner to your significant other, or as a friend to your circle, you can try to find out what makes you happy as a person.

Realize the positive stuff about you by these people who are always looking after you. They're your constant source of energy. Hold them close.

10. Value the People Around you

Talking about having your loved ones and friends around to help you rediscover the good things about yourself, it's important to remember doing the same for them. Respect them by demonstrating how you care, and why you care.

People who give love and who in return are loved never fall victim to the crippling gloom of insecurity. They know exactly what they're worth, and even if they do not feel their best, they trust the people they love will be there to remind them how special they are.

11. Love Yourself

Last but not least, always love yourself. Even if you're in a romantic relationship where you're expected to love someone else, never forget to put yourself in the equation as well.

HOW TO RESOLVE ANY CONFLICT WITH COMMUNICATION SKILLS

Even the happiest of relationships experience conflicts and problems. If handled well, issues provide opportunities for growth in both personal and relationships. Many skills can support people seeking to settle disputes safely. Effective communication is one of the greatest skills which helps in conflict resolution.

Common Disputes

Problems, or disputes, in relationships consist of any circumstance, incident, or experience that affects or matters to those concerned. There are a quite number of factors that lead to conflict, some of which include topics such as finances, children and in-laws, personal issues such as self-esteem, beliefs, aspirations, or priorities, or related issues such as the amount of time together versus time alone, support versus power, affection, and communication. Although there are seemingly endless reasons for conflict, they generally surround all humans' underlying needs, including physical, intellectual, emotional, social, and spiritual. Most significantly, the result is always decided by how we approach and interact with those issues.

Conflicts in Communication

Most people know that we need to communicate on the issue in order to resolve conflicts, but negative communication patterns can often lead to greater frustration and conflict escalation. Consider the following communication challenges:

Body Language/Voice Communication

Tone is more than the words we choose to use. In reality, we sometimes speak our body language and voice tone louder than our words. Shouting, "I'm not angry," for example, is not a very convincing message! If we send an incongruous message where our voice and body language tone is not in line with our message, misunderstanding, and anger sometimes follow.

To surmount this communication challenge, we need to be mindful of what signals our body language and voice tone will convey to others. Speak calmly, give eye contact, a smile if necessary, and maintain an open, relaxed posture.

Differences in Style

Every one of us has a specific way to interact, often

based on interactions with our families, history, gender, and several other factors. For example, when opposed to our partner, we can appear to be more noisy, outgoing, or emotional. While there's no right or wrong style, our past experiences mostly lead to expectations that are not usually communicated verbally with others, which can cause relationship tension and misunderstanding. For instance, if we came from a large family that tended to shout for being heard, we might think it's normal to speak loudly. But if our partner came from a quieter family environment, he/she might be uncomfortable or even scared by an elevated voice.

Discussing our experiences and perspectives will help to explain expectations for ourselves and others and can help our partner appreciate our point of view as well. Knowing this knowledge will also help in the process of problem-solving.

Communication Roadblocks

The roadblocks of communication arise when two people communicate in such a way that none of them feels understood. Research has identified four especially negative communication styles, sometimes referred to as "the apocalypse's four horsemen," because if left unchecked, those interaction styles that gradually become lethal to relationships. Criticism, disdain, defensiveness, and stonewalling are such types.

- **Criticism assails another's character or personality**

While it is common to have concerns about the particular actions of another, because of those actions, it is very different from putting them down as an individual. For example, a complaint may be, "I felt worried when you didn't call me to tell me that you were going to be home late." Criticism can be articulated in the same context as, "You're so unconsidered, you never call me when you're going to be late." Criticism focuses on certain behaviors; criticism focuses negatively on the motives and character of the person.

- **Contempt portrays disgust and disrespect by body language**, such as eye-rolling or sneering, or by name-calling, sarcasm and cutting remarks, to the other person.

- **Defensiveness is an often natural response to criticism and disrespect by individuals, but it also escalates the dispute**.

When we're defensive, we appear to avoid listening to the perspective of the other and shut down contact.

- **Stonewalling withdraws from dialogue and declines to participate in the discussion.**

In other words, it's the adult equivalent of the "silent treatment" that young kids use when upset. Without touch, dispute resolution is unlikely!

Additional examples of communication roadblocks include

- Order ("Quit making complaints!")

- Warning ("If you do that, you will be sorry.")

- Counseling ("You shouldn't behave like that.")

- Recommending ("Wait a few years before you decide")

- Reading ("If you do this now, you're not going to grow up to be a responsible adult")

- Agreeing, only to maintain the peace ("I think you're right")

- Ri. Acknowledging these roadblocks and making attempts to communicate effectively will help individuals resolve roadblocks.

Tips to Resolve Dispute

Ease the Startup.

One of the skills to resolve roadblocks in communication requires a soft start to the discussion by beginning with the constructive, showing gratitude, reflecting on problems one at a time, and taking responsibility for thoughts and feelings. Furthermore, beginning the message with "I" instead of "You" will reduce the defensiveness and encourage positive experiences with others while presenting the issue. For instance, "I want to stay more involved in making money decisions" instead of "you never include me in financial decisions."

Make and Receive Repair Tentative.

Another critical ability in resolving roadblocks in contact is learning how to make and accept attempts at repair. Repair attempts are attempts to prevent an increasingly hostile experience by taking a break or making efforts to calm the situation. This is critical because we often experience extreme emotional and physical stress when disagreements occur, which can impair our ability to think and reason, which can lead to roadblocks in communication. Taking time away from the dispute to calm down (at least 20 minutes) can help us be more prepared to discuss the problem.

Speech and Listening Skills are Important.

It takes good speaking and listening skills to resolve roadblocks in communication. There is a method of speaking-listening to help individuals communicate more effectively. Every partner takes turns to be the speaker and the listener.

The Speaker Rules Include:

1. The speaker should share his/her thoughts, feelings, and concerns—not what he/she thinks the listener's concerns to be.

2. Use "I" statements when you speak, to express

your thoughts and feelings accurately.

3. Keep statements short of ensuring information does not overwhelm the listener.

4. Halt after each short statement so that the listener can paraphrase what has been said to ensure he/she understands, or repeat back in his/her own terms. If the paraphrase is not quite correct, reframe the statement gently again to help the listener understand.

The Listener's Rules Include

1. Paraphrase what the orator says. If vague, request clarification. Proceed until the speaker correctly indicates the message has been received.

2. Don't disagree or give an opinion on what the speaker is saying — wait until you're the speaker, and then do it with respect.

3. The listener should not speak or interrupt while the speaker is talking, except for paraphrasing after the speaker.

In each position, the speaker and listener should take turns so that each has an opportunity to express his/her thoughts and feelings. One can still ask for a time-out. The aim of this activity is not to solve a particular problem, but rather to have a healthy and constructive discussion, and to consider the point of view of each other. While we may not always agree with the other's point of view, understanding and validating the thoughts and feelings of others can improve relationships and help us build on common ground which can lead to more effective negotiation and problem-solving.

HOW YOUR ATTACHMENT STYLE CAN IMPACT YOUR RELATIONSHIPS

Freud understood what he was thinking about (in this case): For better or worse, many assume that in our childhood experiences our adult personalities are unconsciously rooted in. And in our very first relationships, too, the way we relate to others seems to be established — typically with our parents. From the way our caregivers meet our early-life emotional needs, we develop social coping habits that gather into something called "attachment style"— a pattern in how we relate to others. A healthy attachment style could well serve us, fostering solid self-esteem and positive relationships, but an unstable one could hold us back from building functional relationships.

Breaking Attachment Styles

For some time you may have been single, and wonder why. Perhaps you might be a serial dater who gets into relationships that fall hard in the first few months — only to cool down and lose interest. You may want to be in love, but you may find yourself sitting at home watching the GOT. You may have found the perfect partner but get so inside your head that you can't enjoy dinner with them. You may have been in a long-term relationship but feel unfulfilled and you can't seem to trust your partner, no matter what they do. If any of these scenarios apply to you, you can mimic feelings that were created when you were in diapers.

Many of the anxieties, attitudes, and behavioral habits you mimic as an adult are derived from how you felt during the first few years of life. The way that you were connected to your primary caregivers forms our thoughts and acts.

How do we know how well we attached ourselves to our parents as a child? We will probably never really know. What our parents viewed as safe and attentive parenting may not have felt like it to us and what one child viewed as the ideal amount of affection might have felt insensitive to another. However, we should look at our adult actions and deduce that it falls into one of three different categories of attachment.

Many of the anxieties, attitudes, and behavioral habits you mimic as an adult are derived from how you felt during the first few years of life.

Don't get too angry with yourself if you're in a toxic hamster wheel – not entirely your fault. The theory of attachment is useful, especially in identifying insecurities and detachments affecting our general wellbeing. (Not that you should sit around and blame your parents; instead, it is more helpful to use this information to better understand yourself and to help heal any old wounds you have since childhood.) Three key types exist: nervous, avoidable, and secure. There's, of course, a great deal of individual diversity, but most people seem to be identified.

Anxious

People that are anxiously attached need a lot of attention. They never seem to be satisfied with the amount they receive and want more consistently, a need driven by the devastating fear of not being good enough. They often compare themselves to others and strive for perfection, believing that this unattainable state will relieve them of ordinariness — and expendability, somehow.

An anxiously attached person is almost impossible to trust someone entirely, and so they make a mess of romance and friendships. Often they are suspicious, afraid of being betrayed, and predisposed to interfere in others' affairs. They appear to take it personally if you don't write them back in an hour or two; they think something is wrong, they feel irritated, or they fear that they have offended you in some way.

People who are anxiously attached live in their heads, and not in their hearts.

People who are anxiously attached live in their minds and not their souls, causing an extraordinary amount of pain and discomfort. They just don't appear to be getting out of their way. If you can't read their minds, they want more than anyone can give and are offended. They can be cynical about long-term success prospects and prone to temper tantrums. They are always arguing and reluctant to admit their fault.

People who are anxiously attached wait for the other shoe to slip off. They may be constantly on the verge of breaking up with their partner or friends, but because they don't want to be left alone they don't get through with it. So are almost a quarter of all people — does that remind you of anyone?

Avoidant

Another quarter of the world's population falls into the evasive connection group. Such individuals frequently seem oblivious and untouched by even the most tumultuous relationships. They keep their feelings hidden, and do not openly engage in love gestures.

It may seem too dangerous to reveal who they are to outsiders. They also struggle with self-doubt and confusion. They're preoccupied with a large variety of pointless things to separate themselves from others. Often they are workaholics who have no time to socialize with friends and they also seem to neglect their spouses and kids. Avoidants are self-relieving owners, which also leads to relying on unhealthy addictive habits around drugs, exercise, and food.

People who are avoiding may yearn for a romantic relationship but find themselves running from situations where they are being asked to commit —

they cannot give the wind caution, and they struggle with spontaneity even when they see the value therein.

You may have tried to date someone with this type of personality only to be constantly frustrated with their emotional inability to show up. People who are avoiding may yearn for a romantic relationship but find themselves running from situations where they are being asked to commit — they cannot give the wind caution, and they struggle with spontaneity even when they see the value therein. We feel uncomfortable in the face of true intimacy, and appear to slip away when things get intense.

Avoidants are caught up in an unconscious fear of being abandoned and rejected, and therefore do not allow themselves to get too close. This can, unfortunately, lead to solitude, a sense of disconnection, and pessimism.

Rest Assured Safe

And then there are the healthy forms that most of us fall into. Many that are deeply attached find the pleasure in friendships and intimate partners, and are not afraid of letting it hang out. They have — for the most part — a strong and healthy personality, and believe in themselves and the value of companionship. They are looking for partners who are also fit and healthy that will allow them to take risks without fear of failure.

Security relationships are not discouraged when faced with difficulties and can easily be discarded after a breakup. They enjoy rolling their sleeves up and searching for potential solutions to the complex issues that threaten their everyday lives. Instead of internalizing resentments or discomfort, they can speak for themselves. Usually, they are willing to listen to reason and are not threatened by opinions that contrast their own.

Many people that are deeply attached, find the pleasure in friendships and intimate partners, and are not afraid of letting it hang out.

When a securely attached person is coupled with an anxiously or evasively attached person, he/she can immediately tell that something is wrong. This doesn't mean that there are no relationships between these groups but they are sometimes short-lived and unfulfilled if they do. Often securely attached people have a blind spot that stops them from knowing what people with vulnerable attachments deal with. It can be difficult for them to understand the cognitive complexity that occupies the minds of the other classes simply because it makes little sense to them. They are the lucky ones to have had parents who gave them the right amount of affection. This is the primary difference: evaders and nervous types didn't get what they needed to feel absolutely free.

Healing Old Wounds

The specifics of the first years of life are spotty, so we can't go back and fix them, but if you're willing to think beyond the box, there are a few things that can help heal these old wounds.

We also refer to the power of the image. The road between our unconscious state and our conscious mind is surrounded by beautiful images. Intentionally, images arise from our psyche to give us clues as to why we feel a certain way. These are messages from our soul to help us understand better what things require attention and how best to proceed. Just as images drift from the soul, so too will they drift into the psyche from our conscious minds. It is called stimulating the active imagination

One of these imaginations' aims is to communicate with images that can bring us happiness, relax our senses, and give us insight. There is the potential for incredible healing when interacting with photos because there are no past, current, or future limits, and we can construct whatever truth we want. This new awareness produced in an imaginative state is capable of softening the memory meaning and giving us relief. Our older, more seasoned selves can now eradicate the negative self-beliefs, traumas, and fears that we faced as infants. We just need to go back and see our younger self. We have to re-encounter the wounded child inside.

Here's a Guided Imagination to Motivate you:

Find a quiet position in your home or office. Somewhere that the loud traffic noise cannot penetrate. Switch your mobile phone off. Take your shoes and your socks off. Sit back on the board. Give your feet a gentle rub. Stand up straight and head level with your spine.

Now have your eyes closed. Start breathing in deeply. Inhale the nose though. Imagine that all the air you breathe in is packed with affection and compassion.

Imagine all the tension and anxiety leaving your body when you exhale through your mouth. And goodness in there.

76

JEALOUSY IN MARRIAGE AND RELATIONSHIPS: AND WHY DO WE COPE WITH IT?

When do we Become Insecure in Relationships?

I think there are places of persistent weakness in every person. Such vulnerabilities need to be recognized and respected for a marriage to succeed.

This flips jealousy over her head. In relationships, jealousy is becoming an opportunity to connect, rather than something to avoid. Brene Brown writes in her book Daring Greatly: How the Bravery to Be Vulnerable Changes The Way We Live, Love, Parent, and Lead, "Vulnerability is the birthplace of affection, belonging, happiness, confidence, empathy, and creativeness. It is the source of optimism, empathy, responsibility, and honesty. "We can do it in a way that is compassionate and positive when we understand why we are jealous. Recognizing and accepting the inherent vulnerabilities of both your partner and yourself will improve the relationship.

Understand the Causes

Jealousy can be more about your shortcomings in a

relationship than about the actions of your partner. For example, if you've had traumatic experiences in your past you may be inclined to jealousy. It's important to speak about these interactions with your partner, so you can be aware of and appreciate each other's triggers.

Jealousy may be motivated by low self-esteem or a negative image of oneself. If you do not feel attractive and confident, it could be hard to truly believe you love and value your partner. Other times the unrealistic expectations about the relationship can trigger envy. Partners investing 100 percent of their time together is not safe. In Kahlil Gibran's words, "you need spaces together to sustain your bond." Recall that feelings aren't facts. Do you imagine things that actually aren't there? I encourage my clients to ask: "Is that so? "Did this actually happen? If the answer is no, let the negative thoughts run away. Recognize them before actively throwing them off.

Feelings of jealousy can become problematic if they have an impact on your behavior and your feelings towards the whole relationship. Here are some signs of nefarious jealous behavior.

Check your spouse's phone or email without

permission Insult your spouse Assuming your spouse is not attracted to you Grilling your spouse at their place of residence throughout the day Accusing your spouse of lying without evidence If you recognize any of these behaviors in your relationship, seek to understand the vulnerabilities below. I suggest working under the guidance of a Gottman-trained therapist if you need a little extra support doing this. You can find one on the Gottman Referral Network within your area.

Use Jealousy for Good

Using envy in a relationship for positive envy may also be a very real and natural reaction to the actions of your partner. Remember that people have high expectations regarding how they are treated in a good enough relationship. They deserve kindness, compassion, affection, and appreciation to be treated. They expect loyal and honesty on their partner.

If the answer is "Is that so?" "Yes, then telling your partner how you feel before your jealousy becomes resentment is important. Stick to "I" statements when you bring it up and stop saying stuff like "you still" or "you never." Talk about your feelings about the actual situation and make general assumptions about the character of your partner. Say what you need and not what you do not.

For example, "I feel anxious when, when you are out, I don't know where you are or who you are with. I need you to email me, and let me know. "The better your relationship will be, the more you talk. Is there a particular partnership that makes you uneasy? Do you consider that you are stonewalled, or that the conduct of your partner has changed recently?

You and your partner should be transparent about friendships and working relationships with one another and upfront. Transparency helps to make you feel more comfortable. If you're not certain about boundaries, a good thumb rule is to ask yourself, "How would I feel if I heard my partner talking to someone else like this? "If that hurts then a boundary is crossed.

Show each other how much you respect each other by putting your relationship in front of your job, your colleagues and friends. Each time you do this, you build trust.

Through knowing what drives your emotions, and respecting the endearing weaknesses of each other, you can use envy for the better.

Your style of attachment affects important aspects of your intimate relationships with adults, such as engagement, trust, envy, and overall happiness Securely attached people are more likely to feel involved in their relationships, and their relationships appear to last longer. We looked at the four forms of attachment in the previous section.

Let's say you dated someone for three months and things went well. You have a strong connection; you share a sense of humor; you like friends of each other; you didn't see any red flags. You've been with none other on dates for a couple of months now. That person is hanging out at your place one evening and brings up the idea of being exclusive and officially being a couple. What is your reaction to this?

Sure, let's just give her a chance! I like you very

much so let's see where this is heading.

Slow down! I don't see engagement as my thing. We should maybe take a step back.

Wait, so what? My toothbrush is already mounted permanently in your bathroom, you met my parents and you know all my secrets. We have gone "exclusive" way past. Yes. No. No. I don't even ask. Are you insane? I just like you so much. I need some space.

Your response probably depends largely on your attachment style — your thought, feeling, and behavior patterns in the way you connect with others. They typically fall into four distinct styles.

Safe Dismissive-avoidant Anxious-pronounced Fearful-avoidant (a.k.a., disorganized) Of course, various situations affect every relationship. Your response to interaction here will depend on a great many factors. Yet think about all the romantic or other close relationships that you have or are trying to have. Are you seeing the pattern? What about other dimensions, including intimacy, of relationships? Confidence? Is it jealousy? These too are influenced by your type of attachment.

Let's look at a couple of different aspects of

relationships that often determine how they begin, develop, and maybe end.

Commitment

Choosing to engage in a partnership can be a fair, cost-effective method of weighing up the pros and cons. Yet thinking that there are even less moral processes at work is not impossible, too. Including fastener. It's no wonder that out of all the attachment types, people with dismissive-evitable attachment styles are the least committed to their romantic relationship. At the next end of the spectrum, people who are securely affiliated feel the most committed. Researchers who tracked the behavior of people with evasive styles for a couple of months noticed that they were more likely to split up.

Researchers who tracked the practice for a few months of people with avoiding styles noticed they were more likely to have a breakup.

Of course, suffering breakups more often is common for people with avoiding attachment forms. They feel uneasy with emotional closeness and believe that they do not need intimacy or want it. They still congratulate themselves on their needlessness at times. So, the first conflict or downturn in their relationship's levels of excitement might be enough to get them to end it. Alternatively, their unwillingness to commit and get close may push their partner to make the decision.

Envy and Confidence

Envy is a common emotion that we often experience when we are in close relations. The emotion helps us recognize connection risks. When you see your romantic partner flirting with someone else or getting a lot of attention from a possible competitor, it's perfectly normal to become jealous. Jealousy only becomes troublesome when it becomes out of proportion with fact, or contributes to unhealthy behaviors such as controlling your partner intensively or limiting their freedom.

Researchers also found that those with the anxious-preoccupied type of relationship are the most likely to engage in their partners' surveillance.

Researchers also found that those with the anxious-preoccupied type of relationship are the most likely to engage in their partners' surveillance. We even feel worse when we encounter envy than someone without that type of attachment.

On the other hand, when they become jealous, those who are dismissive-avoidant will feel less fearful and sad than other types of attachment. But as opposed to people with stable attachment, both of these unstable attachment types are associated with more irrational trust in a relationship. This is possible because people who are both nervous and evasive have trouble trusting.

Not only can people who are insecurely attached have more envy, but they may also be more likely to jealously make their partners deliberately. In particular, having an anxious-concerned or fearful-evitating style makes a person more likely to induce jealousy. People who are anxiously involved use more direct contact while people who are fearful-evident appear to be passive-aggressive.

Emotional Intimacy

4 prerequisites for being able to have intimacy in a relationship have been described by one attachment

researcher:

Ability to seek care

Ability to give care

Ability to feel comfortable with an autonomous self

Ability to negotiate

These skills are unsurprisingly affected by attachment style. Securely attached people are more linked with their romantic partners, with more relationship commitment, more contact, and more mutual friends. They are even more genuine in the way the relationship expresses itself.

Intimacy of course also extends to platonic relationships. Specifically, another study brought mates into the laboratory to watch them communicate with each other. As "flies on the wall," the researchers did not observe any differences between friend pairs of different types of attachment, but the participants themselves, who were securely attached, felt their conversations involved more sharing and supportive.

Sexual Enjoyment

Securely attached people also have more sexual

intimacy with their partners, with more open sexual communication and more sexual satisfaction overall. Insecurely attached individuals were more likely to have anxiety or inhibitions of interacting with their partners about sex.

In men, having both anxious and resisting forms of attachment is associated with a greater risk of developing sex addiction. Insecure attachment may be the cause of violent actions in women and girls, which helps them to manipulate other people to engage with them without being insecure.

Insecurely attached individuals were more likely to have anxiety or inhibitions of interacting with their partners about sex.

Having a healthy relationship style can be much more than sexual attraction when it comes to loving sex life.

It's obvious there are advantages to having a stable attachment type. In addition to having more healthy and long-lasting romantic relationships, people with safe attachment are more likely to have safer and more rewarding ones as well.

But if you have an insecure style of attachment (through no fault of your own), does that mean you're going to fight intimacy forever? In part three of my mini-series of attachment, we will look at how to overcome insecure attachment through openness, hard work, and a bit of luck.

What can you do to make the relationship more romantic right now?

You could just get a diamond necklace for your wife. Or maybe you should buy her the dream car Mercedes she's always wanted.

It does sound like a good idea, right?

But let's say you didn't ask your wife a question in five years, so you're failing on Love Charts.

Or while you're out with friends on a double date and your wife is starting to tell a story, you're saying, "That's a good story but you're always telling it wrong.

Let me tell you. "So, you fail to show her respect and fondness.

She excitedly plops down on the couch next to you later that night, and shows you a video of a romantic getaway in Italy.

"Is that not romantic? "You answer, are you going to be quiet? I'm just trying to understand this! "And when she wants to communicate with you, you refuse to turn towards her.

Now think back on that necklace and a new car.

Will that resurrect the romance?

I don't believe it.

Possibly she'll throw the necklace to the ground and use the new Mercedes to drive over it a couple of times for good measure.

Love Culture's Micro-Moments have warped what makes a marriage sizzle with passion. Adverts carry the message that a romantic getaway or expensive jewelry is the way to the heart of a woman, but I find the most significant of all the dull moments of relationships.

The micro-moments of love are deeply dramatic. The moment that Jack and Susan have dinner together and talk about their days, instead of watching silent television. Or how Kevin and Kris touch each other tenderly, as they pass through the kitchen.

Love is cultivated during the daily grind. It's the small, seemingly meaningless moments of connection that are the most significant of all.

When we turn to our partner, we build confidence, emotional connection, and a passionate sex life.

As loopy as it might sound, the supermarket's love for romance is heightened. In the seemingly unrelated question about relationships, "do we need milk? "The answer, 'I can't remember that. I'll just catch a couple in case, "makes a lot of difference, rather than shrugging your shoulders nonchalantly.

The number 1 reason for couple fighting is not about money, in-laws, or sex. Most of the complaints in relationships are about the inability to communicate emotionally.

The Emotional Bank Account

Every linked moment in your relationship builds up a love-saving that can be used in tough times.

When a couple has more positive than negative

deposits, they are less likely to mistrust each other during tough times. But if their account with Emotional Bank is in debt of disconnection, then trust and intimacy fade away.

Here are three steps to reconnect when you feel distant from your partner by investing in your Emotional Bank account.

Embrace Offers for Contact

Dr. Gottman says that "couples frequently disregard each other's emotional needs out of mindlessness, not malice." Realizing how important these micro-moments are is the first step to feel more connected with your partner. This is not only important for the confidence in your marriage, but also romance and intimacy.

The simple shift from failing to take for granted everyday interactions can do wonders for a marriage. Helping out with housework is likely to do much more for your relationship than a two week Tahiti break.

We sometimes miss out on bids because our partner is saying it in a negative way. For instance, Kim tells her husband, "It never happens to you to empty a dishwasher, does it? "James is not hearing her offer" (unload the dishwasher please). Instead, the first of the Four Horsemen listens to criticism. When he reacts defensively it is not shocking.

If James had said, "oh, you're OK. I'm sorry, "and then emptied the dishwasher, when she realized her tone was inappropriate, he would have scored brownie points and maybe even a sheepish smile from his wife...

Instead of responding to your partner aggressively, pause for a second, and look behind the words. If you feel that bids in your relationship are constantly wrapped in criticism.

Understand the Love Maps of Each Other

Many couples believe that their partner feels noticed and understood. The key to knowing your partner does not come from reading your mind, but rather from the hard work of putting your partner in a place that they can freely and honestly communicate.

Do you know the fears and pressures your partner is experiencing? What are its aspirations and hopes? What are its priorities this year? Are they different from the previous year?

The secret to knowing each other is: Ask questions

Mind the answers Keep asking questions It is a lifelong process to get to know your partner better and to express your inner self. A dream movie for your partner might not be the same as it was five years ago.

The better the questions that you both make, the greater the emotional investment. If you're looking for suggestions to answer relationship issues, go here.

Develop a Route of Mutual Respect and Gratitude

Remember when the man interrupted his wife and asked her story? Do you think that the relationship built on affection and respect?

We all have personality shortcomings. Instead of targeting the inadequacies of your partner, learn to accept them.

And when you can, your partner's express what you cherish. The idea is to get your partner to do it right and say, "thank you for doing it. I found that you emptied the dishwasher, and I really appreciate it." Your wife feels an emotional bond every time you do so. As a result, you're putting your emotional gains into the Emotional Bank account of your relationship.

Love isn't focused on the major holidays or lavish on presents. Probably the most important of these are the seemingly meaningless moments of communication.

When can you get the passion back in a relationship?

It's complicated and a long hard road without quick fixes, but there are some sure things you can do to recover a partner's attention, whether it's a long-term boyfriend or a new one. It happens to the best of us — that certain point when something seems to break, and you know the relationship has become boring, and the deep love that you have now become just a friendship with one another. You're happy to be together, but you're not exactly passionate about it.

All is brand new when we start a relationship, so the feelings that you experience are enthralled and fill you with joy. However, it's normal that those feelings start to dissipate after a certain period of time. Even though you still feel something in your life towards the main squeeze, love no longer encompasses everything. So when a coupling reaches that stage, how do you regain love?

Step One: In Order To Go forward, Take a Step Backward

Try to remember what the first few days, weeks, or even years were like (if you're lucky). Tell yourself what you have done differently, and how you have treated one another. So then try to relive those times, with the help of your boyfriend or husband. Go to a nice fancy restaurant again on a first date, and maybe order the same meals you'd eat back then. Recover Love and Passion! Forget about calories and kids for one hour, and save the week! In trying to trigger your mind in remembering how you felt about someone and why you felt the way you once felt, these little things can be very important.

Step Two: Compromise, compromise, compromise, compromise!

Compromise: It's a crucial word and one I can't worry enough about. Compromise: Compromise! You probably know when your significant other will react to anything at this point in your relationship, or when he'll want to engage in an activity that you don't have any interest in. You're going to create a fast response system to combat these things: "No, I don't want to do this" or "We're going to the dinner party, whether you like it or not." These kinds of stock responses are not conducive to a good, happy relationship and can stop your relationship from regaining love. Instead, think carefully about your answer to one of the requests from your partner, take a moment to consider and think about what he is asking, and offer a simple, calculated response. Hopefully, you will learn to agree on certain issues over time, and if he wants the relationship to go on and your love to come back to him, then he will realize that and reply. Even if you disagree on something, or say no, before responding, the fact that you considered a reply will do you a world of good. And yeah, you might enjoy some of the things that you'd never done before!

Step Three: Make new fates, and get more of a life outside.

You have to widen your horizons first in order to reclaim love because the man in your life starts to crave attention. You'll enjoy your time together, even more, when you're spending time apart! Such external interests could be something you find fascinating (except of course an affair) or you've always wanted to check it out. If you have kids, get to know and spend some time with other parents. If you'd like to get fit, enter a gym and start exercising your body for yourself, not him.

You may have also dreamed of spending time drawing, or some other artistic pastime. This is your chance to get it done! Such acts all have something in common — your man in these projects will join you. If he does, then you might find a shared love for a hobby or skill, as well as spending some extra quality time with each other. If he doesn't at least, you'll start to be happier with your new life, and it's easier to regain love all around when a person's happier.

Step Four: Don't have games to watch.

I'm not speaking of Monopoly or Scrabble! The mind games and digs at each other must be avoided. You might feel justified in what you say or do in one of these verbal fights, but over time they not only wear you out but they also destroy the desire of your partner to be with you. Start to be honest with each other instead of beating around the bush and making snide remarks. Mind games can be enjoyable, and –in certain cases— harmless, like teasing in the bedroom or playing combat. In reality, these can help build a successful relationship, and be healthy reminders why you love one another. The petty arguments that can start creeping into a relationship after a while, however, do little to help you start regaining love as you did when you first met. Doing things or saying "to get back" at somebody will always lead to regret.

Step Five: Be frank.

Honesty — a simple term, but perhaps the most important element of a relationship, and an integral part of restoring love that may have fallen away. I'm sure that at some stage in your relationship, when nothing appeared to be taboo, you were frank and you could tell your partner everything there was to know about yourself. Things change as we evolve, and two things do happen.

First of all, you will feel more relaxed with your significant other, and you would be able to talk about stuff that would have humiliated you beforehand. The second thing that happens, though, is that you begin to feel uncomfortable telling him certain information, such as about a co-worker who hits you or you've been feeling sexual repression.

You consciously overlook things because you don't want to hurt feelings. It might not be big, but all these little lies and dishonesty can end up costing your life together. Try to be 100 percent open with your partner instead. You will find each other opening up together, and as well as cultivating a love for each other, it will also help you chat, and connect.

Step Six: Just trust each other.

Following on from the last step and working hand in hand with it, the key to a lasting bond of love is confidence. If you're not trusting your partner, then love isn't obvious. Distrustful thoughts overtake us if we allow it to. It will be an uphill battle to restore love without first regaining trust, and so start working through your anxious feelings as soon as possible. Ask yourself why you lost your once-held faith in your man, and what you or he could do to regain that, and make things right again.

Step Seven: Contact is paramount.

Communication, along with honesty and confidence, is one of those main elements in regaining love, and is necessary for any drive to rekindle a connection. Honestly and honestly speak to each other about the weather, the new American Idol, and the movie you'd like to see. Ask him how his day went at work, and tell him what yours was like. Although it may seem obvious, it's shocking how many couples are refusing to just sit down and speak to each other. Small transformations will help you open the doors to the main topics you need to think about.

Step Eight: get the spark back again.

On the second first date, you were out, had your meal, and are now sitting, sipping wine. Don't let the night and closeness stop there, then hold your hands, brush your hair from your face, and usually give the guy you love a mess. He may need to be supportive, particularly if he's out of the habit of doing the same, but if he's once a romantic young man, he still has it in him, it just needs coaxing out.

If you make the first move, you're never sure where the evening could end! Romance is, in general, necessary for regaining love in your relationship. This and the other steps mentioned provide a very good structure in which to recover love in the relationship you do not want to end. Teamwork is important as in all things so get your partner with the program on board. If he is not willing or unable to do so, then maybe it is time to look for a new partner who understands your love's needs better.

SELF PUBLISHER

KÖRMÖCZI AGNES